W9-CYH-017

A BABY STARTS TO GROW

THIS IS A LET'S-READ-AND-FIND-OUT SCIENCE BOOK

A BABY STARTS TO GROW

By Paul Showers
Illustrated by Rosalind Fry

Thomas Y. Crowell Company   New York

LET'S-READ-AND-FIND-OUT SCIENCE BOOKS

Editors: *DR. ROMA GANS*, Professor Emeritus of Childhood Education, Teachers College, Columbia University
DR. FRANKLYN M. BRANLEY, Astronomer Emeritus and former Chairman of The American Museum-Hayden Planetarium

*Available in Spanish

ISBN 0-690-11319-6
0-690-11320-X (LB)

4   5   6   7   8   9   10

When this baby was one day old, he weighed seven
pounds.
He was twenty inches long from the top of his
head to the tip of his heels.

When he was one year old, he weighed twenty-one
   pounds.
He was thirty inches long, and everybody said:
"My, how he has grown!"

Babies grow before they are born, too.

    Before a baby is born, it grows inside its mother's body.

    It grows in a hollow place called the uterus, or womb.

    It grows a hundred million times bigger than it was when it began.

At first there is no baby at all.

Then two very small cells join together.

One is called the sperm. It comes from the father.

The other is called the ovum. It is inside the mother.

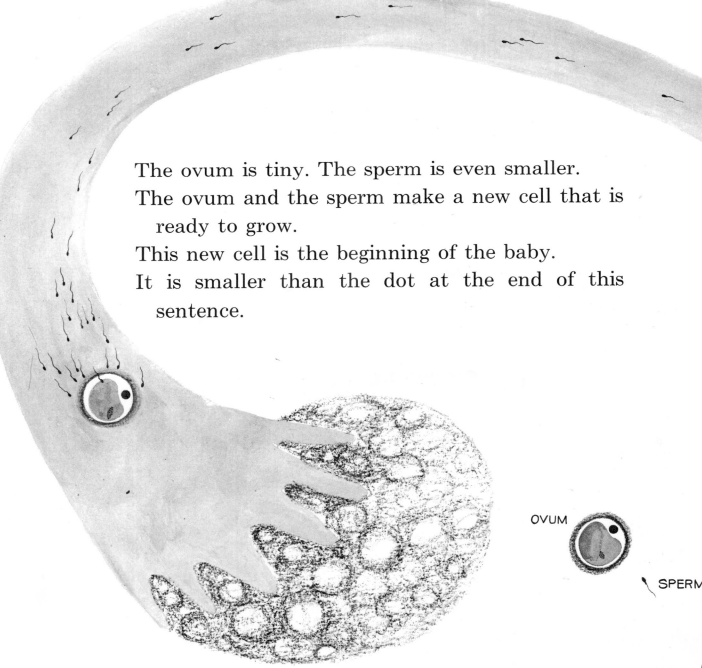

The ovum is tiny. The sperm is even smaller.
The ovum and the sperm make a new cell that is
   ready to grow.
This new cell is the beginning of the baby.
It is smaller than the dot at the end of this
   sentence.

OVUM

SPERM

After a day or so this new cell divides.
Now there are two cells.
The cells keep on dividing—
four cells—
eight cells—
more and more cells.

After a few days there is a tiny ball of cells.
It is hollow inside. The hollow is filled with water.
The little ball fastens itself to the inside of the
mother's uterus.

9

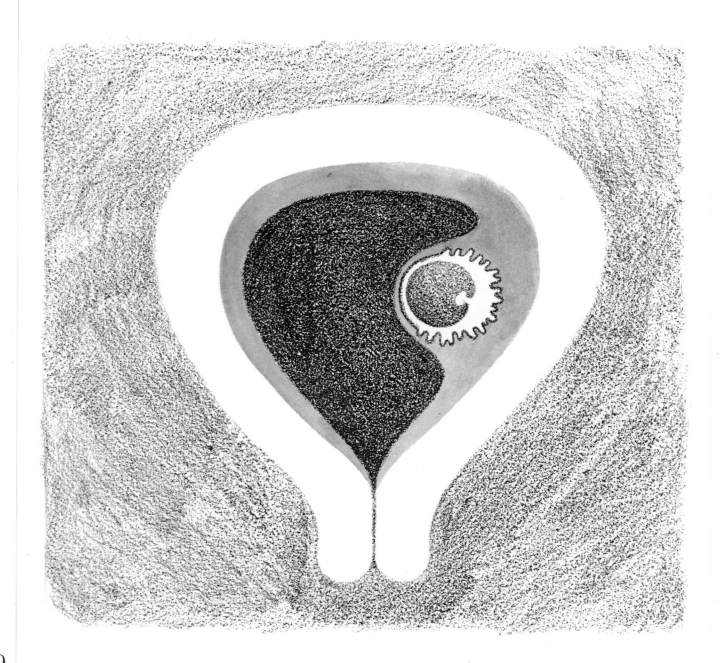

The ball is still very small, but it keeps growing.
   Thousands and thousands of new cells are made—
      millions and millions of new cells.
   The cells become different parts of the growing ball.

A thick stalk begins to grow in the water inside
   the ball.
   It grows out from one side of the ball.
   There is a lump at the end of the stalk.
   This lump is the baby.
   It doesn't look much like a baby.
   It looks like a very small bean.
   There is water all around it.

The baby is still very tiny.
   After four weeks the ball and the baby inside it
are exactly this big.

But a baby grows fast.

In five weeks it is almost twice as big as it was the week before.

Now it has eyes and the beginnings of arms and legs.

In three more weeks fingers and toes begin to grow.
So do the ears.
Inside its body, the baby's heart is beating.
It moves the baby's blood through its body.
It moves the blood down into the stalk and back
again.

16

A baby needs food and oxygen to make it grow.
We get oxygen from the air we breathe.
The baby cannot eat or breathe inside the ball
   of water.
It does not need to.
Its mother eats and breathes for the baby.

When the mother eats, the food is digested in her
stomach.

Then it goes into her blood.

When she breathes, oxygen from the air goes into
her blood, too.

In the mother's uterus, her blood flows around the
ball with the baby inside it.
The food and oxygen pass from the mother's blood
through the side of the ball into the stalk.

Inside the stalk the baby's blood takes in the food
and oxygen.
The blood carries food and oxygen up the stalk
and to every part of the baby's body.

A baby grows very fast with the food and oxygen
   it takes from its mother.
After four months it is about eight inches long
   and it looks like a baby.
The ball full of water has stretched like a bal-
   loon.
The stalk has become a long, thick cord.
It is fastened to the middle of the baby.

The baby floats in the water inside the ball.
The water is like a cushion.
It keeps the baby from bumping its head or its knees or elbows.

After five months the baby can move its hands and
   feet.
   Its eyes are still shut. It can suck its thumb.
   Sometimes its mother can feel it kicking.

As the weeks go by, the baby becomes bigger and
   stronger.
   The ball of water grows bigger, too.
   The ball pushes against the sides of the uterus.
   The mother's stomach sticks out more and more.

At the end of nine months the baby is strong
enough to live outside its mother's body.
Its eyes are ready to open and see.
Its ears are ready to hear.
The baby is ready to be born.

29

It comes slowly out of its mother's body into the world.

The cord is still fastened to the baby.

The doctor ties a string around the cord. He cuts the cord.

The place where the cord was fastened to the baby is the baby's belly button.

The baby doesn't need the cord any more.
  Its lungs are ready to breathe air.
  Its stomach is ready to digest food.
  The baby is ready to begin to live a life of its
    own.

33

ABOUT THE AUTHOR

PAUL SHOWERS is a newspaperman and writer. His first job was with the Detroit *Free Press;* later he worked on the New York *Herald Tribune.* During World War II he served in the Air Corps for a year, then joined the staff of *Yank*, the Army weekly. Since the war, with the exception of a brief stint with the New York *Sunday Mirror*, he has been on the staff of the Sunday *New York Times.*

Mr. Showers was born in Sunnyside, Washington, received his B.A. degree from the University of Michigan, and now lives with his family in suburban New Jersey.

ABOUT THE ILLUSTRATOR

ROSALIND FRY has lived in and traveled through most of her native Australia. Born in Brisbane, Queensland, she lived on a farm in Armidale, and then during World War II, journeyed 2,500 miles across the desert to Perth in Western Australia. She later moved to Melbourne and now lives in Sydney with her husband and five children.

A recipient of a diploma of illustration from Australia's National Art School, Miss Fry is a well-known illustrator. Her pictures have appeared in several books published both in the United States and abroad.